Joe the Ghost

For information, permissions or ordering bulk orders, email:

Editor@middlecreekpublishing.com

ISBN: 978-1-957483-02-3

Joe the Ghost

POEMS

CHRIS RANSICK

Middle Creek Publishing & Audio, LLC.
Beulah, CO USA
↑

Praise for Joe the Ghost

In *Joe the Ghost*, Chris Ransick's narrator speaks from what the Celts call the "thin place," a world between corporeal and spirit. From his transcendent perspective, Joe fully inhabits his earthly body and its delights, yet simultaneously leaves them far behind. *"Everyone is dying but only some / also live,"* he tells us—a wisdom borne of both the poet's tender care and brilliant craft. This is a soaring collection, the work of a master who left us at the pinnacle of his powers. As Ransick writes, *"I forgive I forgive I forgive myself for the / song I ran out of time to sing."* These poems will continue to sing long after we, too, are out of time.

    —Joy Roulier Sawyer, author of *Lifeguards* and *Tongues of Men and Angels*

Chris Ransick was my good friend. I knew him in Colorado and on the Oregon coast, where we had both moved for personal reasons. I have never seen a poet grow by such leaps as Chris accomplished in the last two years of his short life, and these final books, *Temporary House* and *Joe the Ghost,* catch him at his best, darkly funny, humane, eager for life. He once told my students that poetry was the antidote to the mediocrity and dreck of ordinary life. His conversation was like that, like music, reaching into joy. I miss him terribly.

    —David Mason, former Colorado Poet Laureate, author of *Ludlow: A Verse Novel*

Only a few strong poets—Keats comes to mind—have had the ability and courage to look their own approaching death in the eye and craft memorable work not only in spite of that fact, but also out of it. Chris Ransick belongs in this company. To have known and loved Chris makes Joe the Ghost almost unbearable, but it is also unbearably beautiful, a joyous, painful and profound meditation on the end of life and the ends of life by a poet who was taken from us, at the height of his powers, far too soon. I am grateful to have known Chris and to be haunted from this day forward by Joe the Ghost, who speaks "the necessary wisdom that always goes unheard."

    —David J. Rothman, author of *My Brother's Keeper*, Colorado Book Award Finalist, former Poet Laureate of Colorado's Western Slope, former Resident Poet of Colorado Public Radio.

Chris Ransick's *Joe the Ghost* expresses the author's direct confrontation with mortality. Death is *"shrinking/ to enter his navel."* Joe the Ghost *"will never be whole again."* Despite this grim reality there is a celebration of the natural world and even the process of decay, *"knowledge of/ sun built the cells of everything."* One can feel the poet's close attention and love for the world. We can see beauty and acceptance in this stunning collection. There is no heaven, no eternal living, only singing.

    —Sheryl Luna, author of *Magnificent Errors*, Seven, and *Pity the Drowned Horses*.

I do not have the words to prepare a reader for the impact of reading the soaring yet gentle farewell embodied in Chris Ransick's poetry collection *Joe the Ghost*. The art that poet's practice allows for an occasional definitive statement on leaving, but in this book, we actually get an entire collection built to pass on all the warmth and wisdom that this great poet possesses. Read this book, soon—it's that important.

    —J Diego Frey, author of *Umbrellas or Else* and *The Year the Eggs Cracked*

for the beloved

)

I have this that I must do . . .
I must go down with the poor
Purse of my body and buy courage,
Paying for it with the coins of my breath.

—RS Thomas

Could it think, the heart would stop beating.

—Fernando Pessoa

CONTENTS

Joe the Ghost Gets Diagnosed

Out of the swamp it comes, darkly hung
with sodden weeds, muck-painted to
hide its shape. The sharpened teeth

stay concealed for later use. Joe's been
sunning himself in the tall grass,
lying naked and warm in liquid light,

which disappears all at once, as if the
thickest cloud suddenly coalesced
above. Out of the swamp lumbers this

beast. It moves slowly because nobody
outruns it, ever. Its impossibly silent
approach is necessary, a mystery

until it isn't. In his imperfect reverie,
planning a future he won't reach,
Joe is oblivious. It closes in, shrinking

to enter his navel, wince-wince.
It will make a home in him. It will
eat the joy right out of his belly

in small bites, leaving a husk. He will
never be whole again. The lost years,
which didn't exist, now will certainly not.

He'll set off through the swamp on a
listing raft, his memories yellowing,
dropping away. His lover will leave

because she must, she has no choice.
His children will grieve longest. He is not
yet, but he will become echoes and dust.

Joe the Ghost Takes the Train up the Coast

Portland's stained facades are
hung with mist. Sane and insane

denizens mingle, indistinguishable
until struck with rare shafts of sun.

What does the stooped mumbler
need to say so badly she's chosen

scampering ants for an audience?
Joe wants to kneel beside her

and ask what she knows, but this
is human touch, which he must

relinquish, if not the desire for it.
In Union Station, the broad

wooden bench is made for ghosts.
A little boy sits next to him, eyes

big as pennies, takes tiny bites of a
flopping ham sandwich, casts

quick shy glances at Joe, wondering
if the transparent man

is about to cry for the same reason
as him. Above them both, the

the big, beautiful clock terrifies him
in ways it did not yesterday.

Ghost Nocturne 1

Rain too soft to make a sound begins
past midnight, but who knows when.

As you sleep, you don't always dream
and what comes between scenes is a

warm breath on your skin from eternity.
Joe the Ghost wakes and his face

is wet, but it isn't the rain and he
won't sleep again. How long an hour

becomes when you hang off its edge
above an abyss, arms growing weaker

and resolve dissolving. Under the arched
fronds of a sword fern, some creature

shivers and can't contain its grief, gives
just one note to the night but my, my,

how its vast hollow tone hints at all things
lived and forgotten, suffered and fallen

mute. It's not even winter yet, but tall
Sitka spruce shudder at alders already

giving up, going yellow, denuding
themselves like they always do at the

first hint of hardening darkness. Joe would
join them, drop down at the mouth

of the spring, ask its cold flow to rinse
flesh from bone, slip the mind from its

mooring, help his spirit deliquesce.
But no, he'll stay beside the sleeper,

with her body so warm, with his hands
that can't stop touching, not just yet.

The Crying Time

Ghost tears, weightless, rise
from his eyes. Clouds form

from these so now you know
how much is all the world's

sorrow. Joe holds his ghostwife,
awake all night, the dreams

he can no longer own dissolve
in September rain and

run down window glass.
The gentle doe that creeps

into his garden with her
broken-legged fawn pauses

by the pond and patiently
hopes for him to become

like her, soft on the Earth,
insistent to live, but ready

to flee. The owls have already
conferred and agree to

serve as sentries, perched on the
alder's thickest branch, to chase

away devils. Crow won't cry over
Joe's fate, but just this once declines

to taunt him, he who will never
feel as deeply as the forest.

Joe the Ghost in the Spiderweb

Spun silver strands in yellow sun, intricate
and geometric, strong for the purpose, but
fragile to human hands. The web billows in
breezes, a torn sail straining, refusing to break.
Joe draws close enough to find a delicate
creature, entrapped, latticed wings
more sheer than a memory of summer's
last warm night. How much fear can
a winged fairy feel and isn't it finally the
flavor of it, not the size. He raises his finger,
then lowers it, unsure whether to leave the
frantic flyer for the spider or cheat that
architect, gathered into herself in a corner,
hungry as him and guilty of nothing.
Come morning, the prisoner still
struggles. The spider is dead, not patient.

Joe the Ghost and the Angry Breakers

The disorganized sea churns, waves moving in
several directions, overtopping others thick
with sand by the time they splay out, exhausted
on the strand. Murres made for angry oceans
ride frothy flats, dive under crashing rims,
feed in rough water. In his imagination, Joe
drowns a half mile out, cold to his bones so
surrender hurts less and takes less time. Peace
for him, grief for them, stealing only from
scientists to whom he promised his fascinating
guts. There will be no more books. There will be
no more books. Tiny crabs will feed in his skull
where poems coalesced and slowly his clothes
will dissolve. His shoes might rest, tongues
animate in current, speaking for a while his
last wise remarks. The ones he didn't wear
will end up on a rack in a secondhand store
until a traveler puts them on and is seized
with an urge to recite Macbeth's soliloquy.
After an inappropriate interval, another man
will slip into his bed and stain the sheets,
stinking of mediocrity, but still able to steal
the jewel. His molecules will be distributed
and Joe will finally learn to haunt the spaces
where his joy used to be, fashioning from
longing an afterlife, singing sorrows all night
without making a sound on the sea floor.

Ghost Nocturne 2

The soft sea floor receives
the gray whale without needing
a language to explain.

The diaphanous forest insect
that lives only ten days
sticks in the house spider's web

on day one and is dismissed as a
small loss, which any ghost knows,
misses the whole point.

Crow needs few words to mock
the crushed squirrel carcass
before pecking at its guts.

Let this be an example to us all,
but especially to poets. Say what needs
saying and not a word more.

In the morning, sated slugs
big as cigars cling to the rhubarb
they denuded in a night reverie.

Isn't there enough death
in the dank forest to keep them
busy? Finally, fire will

dance in his ribs until ash,
they collapse. It's how ghosts
are born and return without voice.

Joe the Ghost Spacewalks

Tethered and mumbling poem shards,
half-awake between dawn and night's
second nightmare, Joe rises to test thin
legs against gravity—either it's zero or
the opium has made him weightless.
He crosses the carpet, a warm mossy pier,
gooseflesh rippling up his back, cinching
his robe against the absolute cold of space,
the only place you can float. Fifty years ago,
falling from the pear tree, he learned
how gravity takes you quick, as do facts.
Even in the warm sea off Napali
he could have let himself sink, follow
the turtle deeper. He can't remember but
assumes the womb was tight around his
limbs. He's about to abandon ship
when the sky clears above the Sitkas and
starlight turns the pond platinum,
certain waves having traveled so far
they are all that remains of their star.

Joe the Ghost at the Mouth of the Mine

Negative space is purple black
and pulsates. Dead man's tongue

licks Joe's neck just as he falls
asleep. At the mine's mouth, only

crow does not desert him,
cawing from slagged rocks piled

tenser than the angle of repose.
Bottoms of clouds blister

and dusk's falling temperature
makes the fake cave moan,

Plutonian breath of chilled mud
and surrender. Joe knows

where the downslope leads,
chasing silver to the stone

that never yields, even as the
way back collapses behind him.

Joe the Ghost Sings with the Psithurism

Joe lay awake and wished all night
until dawn-hushed fears, soaked in
pale morning moon's cool light,

felt like well-worked leather, broken in.
He wanted to sleep in the forest of dreams,
but kept waking up in the real woods

where one's visions are just what they seem.
What the wind does is its own business
and it will not behave, no matter

the headland it presses against, shredded
on the limbs of ancient Sitka or toppling
such a tower, mother to the whole slope.

It wails and makes a melody ghosts can't
resist so he opens his throat, harmonizes,
and in this way forgets his slow fade.

Joe the Ghost's Recurring Vision of the Leaving

She is most beautiful walking away.
Joe's always known this, confirmed
on a thousand streets. Even in Paris

when she left to get a lemonade
from the street vendor's cart, it was
tragic. In Denver, down the sloping lawn

with their daughter, he saw the distant
slack river suddenly churn in rapids.
In the Burren, she navigated slabs

of karst until she slid into
a crevasse and wildflowers
sprung up from the place.

In an unfamiliar mountain town, she
slowly disappeared in swirling snow,
walking backward, away from him.

Once, as they threaded a path among
Icelandic thermal pools, slow mists
obscured her shape when he stooped

to tie his bootlace. No matter how often
it happens, when she fades from view,
it's the last time and she's beautiful.

Joe the Ghost Meets His Unmaker

Its teeth cannot be seen, buried
already in flesh. The language
is all vowels, which works for moans
if you stick to verbs. The hill
to the house of this god is steep
past cairns of skulls. Once there,
he will unpack the fears
no one voices and hang them up
to wear again tomorrow. Once there,
he will eat his regrets without
sauce, drink denial from
a goblet shaped like doubt.
His Unmaker has studied long
hours to find the best seam to
rip first. The pillow where Joe
rests his head will be used
in evidence against him.
His favorite shirt will be given
to another man. The friendly dog
that licks every hand will
bite his. The house has clocks
without hands, though they never
stop ticking. There's a box
for complaints by the door
and it's full of tears and ashes.

Joe The Ghost Drinks the Deadly Thing

The nurse's hands are miniature
which makes the needle sharper.
In a chilly room, she searches for an
invisible vein in his arm and it keeps
hiding in dark folds of muscle until
she closes her eyes and presses
fingers gently on his former flesh.
Friends packed a barrel of courage,
rolled it into his chest while he slept,
anticipating even small fears like this,
so, he taps it and waits for the rush.
Everyone is dying, but only some
also live. Without a voice now, he can't
warn them. The loyal dogs he loved
and buried come one by one
into the room and nuzzle his hand,
licking away the salt and searching
his face with bottomless brown eyes.
Suddenly, she finds the vein and
punctures it and the poison, that is
also medicine, flows. There is no way
back, only forward into foreignness.

Ghost Nocturne 3

Does the forest ever sleep? Vining plants
grow best in darkness, pausing

in daylight to unfurl glossy spades
and drink deep, but come dusk

they turn relentless in reaching,
entwining, colonizing. Tendrils

spread over decayed forms, life
devolving into duff. A legion of

slugs rise out of hiding and gnaw
blindly at whatever is most alive,

but will settle for rotted things
chanced upon in shadows.

Into this alien world, the mind
projects itself as if a visitor, not

a participant. A bare foot's fine
architecture will shed its flesh

and reveal remarkable bones,
the work of eons, ephemeral.

Joe the Ghost Awakes in His Body Again

The hot cramp starts as a knot in a wire,
marble sized and taut from his front rib
to spine, but at least not running through
his heart. What is that taste at the back
of his throat—battery acid cut with
sour milk and longing. But the sun blazes
in the canyon's crowns and three
hummingbirds slash and fight for
sole possession of the feeder with
three perches. They are beautiful
despite their fury, iridescent green bellies
and tongues flickering from long beaks.
Joe's back in the real world, he knows,
when he tests his fingers and they still
burn. The black homunculus still chews
in its nest. His nation faces its own
cruelty day after day, dissolving itself.
Gulls of hate cruise shell middens dotted
with kids' bloody backpacks. Joe proceeds
to his sack of pills and buries his face
until sated, sedated. His thirst is fissured
and has a personality, obnoxious at dawn.
All Joe's friends, the true and kind, send
soft rockets skyward as the stars fade
and hope he will see them arc. Even if
they burst into flames, as some do,
there's no fault in spending your love
all at once, even if no one is watching.

Joe the Ghost Counts His Bulletholes

1

Laparoscopes pierce and leave
neat entry wounds, mere
slits in skin no wider than

fingernail marks death makes,
impatient lover who, in thrall,
gets too good a grip.

2

Ghosts feel no physical pain,
but their memories are flawless,
vivid and real as lived.
In this way, the kiss at dusk
on the cliff, hair damp with
sea mist and blown across her
warm lips, is enough of heaven.

3

Anesthesiologist.
Pancreatic specialist.
A surgeon named Themistocles.
Nurse, nurse, intern, nurse,
gentle hands turning the
pain's hammerhead to fog.

4

They run a camera down his throat,
another up his ass. Joe once had a lousy job,
but it never came to this.

5

The world inside us a mystery,
a multiverse too vast to grasp,
density, distance, invisible forces,
consciousness and its absence,
imagination the great spirit
eternity gives and retrieves.

Sunset Is Not Less Beautiful to Ghosts

The last rays of a perfect day
passing between his ribs are
liquid and wave, warmth and melt.

The sun heals what it kills
as it does. To whom will he bequeath
his joy since he can't keep

having it? Who deserves his enormous
grief and would giving be unkind?
Seagulls circle, awaiting him

at the landfill, except those sure
calling him by his secret name
as he sits on the beach is better.

Make of me an anemone,
Joe begins to pray. Let my meaty
mouth open to the ocean's

accident, that I may eat again
like any hungry creature. I will
fix myself in the groin of a

rock only sometimes submerged
and learn the color of cold
shallows so I may be aqua

and softly receptive in a sunset
such as this, lit briefly on the
horizontal at low tide.

Joe the Ghost Goes to the Forest to Heal

He no longer sees the forest as trees, having learned to look to
what's fallen and teems with life, the nurse-logs returning
to earth, dissolving to duff deep enough to swallow him.
A million nameless creatures traverse fallen salal leaves and
Joe lays down his body there, hoping with patience to
become it. He keeps his dreams in a hollow stump
moss overgrows so their glow warms Sulphur Tufts
that burst upward overnight and into October sun,
lemony nipples dangerous and lovely. In stillness,
he inhales spruce and fir exhalations, soft air candied
with greenery and salted with sea. The Stellar's jay's
arrogance is earned by a singular blueness as he raids.
All the invisible worms are on his side and will wait.
The tiniest of spiders eats her own web at dusk and by dawn
has spun another more elegant than anything he'll make.
None of these creatures expects to live long nor wastes
a thought on it, and none writes poems. Nothing
in the forest is a symbol. It's all real and incessantly
shifting, never a surface still. No promise has ever been
broken by a forest that never makes one. Knowledge of
sun built the cells of everything and is the only thing
worth believing. This is the lesson for Joe, how to heal.

Ghost Nocturne 4

If night must come, soften it with rain and
the scent of licorice ferns growing from

the torn throats of fallen firs. Let no light
pass through clouds between him and stars

he thought he owned until he learned
they burned away so long ago, leaving

only their last poems to ride out the
vastness toward him. Joe will trade nothing

he has now for anything to come. He must
empty his body of love, and will comply

until he collapses, an exhausted star.
The spring was still trickling last time

he listened and the owls still fly in silence,
hunting onyx seams in a forest absorbing him.

If they want to cry that two-note song
from the alders, he will harmonize

if only he finds just the tone. It may
take eternity and Joe at least has that.

Joe the Ghost Combs His Hair

At dawn I sighed to see my hairs fall;
At dusk I sighed to see my hairs fall.
For I dreaded the time when the last lock should go…
They are all gone and I do not mind at all!

Po-Chu-I,
832 CE

Predawn rain on the pond is the sound of wishes
that might yet come true. Joe thinks of every
bird huddled in the canopy, soaked and chilled to its
hollow bones. The alders bow to dormancy, drop
pale leaves to the soaked earth, already plotting
to burst green again from the same limbs. Spring
is a rumor in November, reliable though it
never arrives as expected. Joe knows well how
winter's long corridor of dark afternoons make
whatever you carry heavy. He steps from the bed
and takes up his burdens, shivers as a prayer to his
devils, and steps, feet tingling, over ice-white tiles
to the sink. As a ghost, he only appears in mirrors
at night, so this is his chance and it's waning.
Newly chiseled from living form, he's lean and pale as
a trout's belly, hair the color of smoke off tinder.
His brushstrokes each bring a nest of it down,
tangled skeins sloughed to the porcelain. He
was warned in the hospital's shiny brochure.
If he never believed in ghosts, he cannot now
begin to believe in himself, though the strands
stuck to his hands are proof he's still in the room,
as is his woman, whose soft breathing sings
from the heat of the bed he's just left. This, too,
is a way of being alive, the haunting of spaces
where your joy was. Joe stands naked at the
rain lashed window and lets slow dawn erase him.

Joe the Ghost Takes His Medicine

In a devil's garden grow the edible violets
that burn his veins. Joe sits under an arbor
of snakes in the place marked for him.

Soft hands will bring him blankets and pills, but first
they spike his chest and open the drip,
they work to kill the thing, but not kill him.

In a lab, his blood is pulled apart for secrets,
the soup unmade back to ingredients.
An unseen hand in a sterile field will reveal

who's winning and losing, whether surgeons
will dull their scalpels on his ribs.
What a massacre that will be. Joe wants to

rise from that torn place, but no guarantees
will be given, only art and compassion.
Split, gouged, and stapled, he may wake

on a sun-warmed boulder in a slow, green river,
but probably not. Make it a nest of machines if
that's the way out, back to the arms of the beloved.

Joe the Ghost on Cape Perpetua's Cliffs

Lymphocytes and platelets low, he's stoned
on his sickness, sleeve of his body toxic to his love.
Joe walks with her up the high trail, surf loud
in a slow way well before it's seen. November sun
aslant and pure, warms his face, healing kisses
and whispers off the tongue of a goddess.
Joe wants to cheat and fly off the precipice,
reclaim his former life as a falcon, brief
though it was. There will be no more
flying and he knows she is already leaving,
but it will take all the rest of his time.

Joe the Ghost Enters Sempiternity

Under a waxing gibbous bright enough to
glint on the ferns' swords and throw long thin
shadows past the water skeeters on their
silvery pond surface, Joe steps into sempiternity.
How his legs shiver and his breath coils
in his lungs. After all the education and whisky,
he expected this, but ghosts, not men, most need
forgiveness and cannot have it. So haunting
happens inside time but for an indefinite term.
All Joe wants to ask is why the grief with teeth
had to start before death—but ask whom?
Since no answer ever speaks from the woods,
all answers there lie hidden. The owl's silence
is never accidental, nor the worm's. Inside
time, things don't end, they only change form,
matter separating and reassembling in shapes
that never resemble former selves and which
remember nothing. Under an alder, leaves
gather and shift loyalty from tree to soil.
Rain falls, creek swells, down to the sea to be
subsumed and to spew from the grey whale's
blowhole. Joe hopes his body, like the rain,
went for something noble like that, but
he might be scattered across a billion grains
of sand, settling for a murky view of forever.

Joe the Ghost Grows Visible in Darkness

Ghosts exist only in present tense, at the
mouth of the woods, in mist the ocean mills

from churned surf, salted and backlit.
All sleepers forget the sea never ceases

its trade with the beach, but only ghosts know
the winter strand's silver is pure radiance

and even they cast shadows in such light,
defined in every curve. Joe gives the beached

sea lion a wide berth, but his dark inverted
self comes too close. Her flinch, familiar,

echoes in him and his weak fingers
and burnt tongue fumble, mumble

a troubling loss of dexterity and language,
merely the flesh succumbing to time. This

was to be expected, but how does one face
disappearing in daylight, when a lover

turns her face from the space you inhabit
invisibly? Joe wants her to wait for dusk

and what follows, for the inked sky to scatter
its white fires that map the firmament.

Then he will come to her. Then he will
bring back his body to again be hers,

and when he does, all that's left is the
scent of her skin and even that, dispersing.

Ghost Nocturne 5

It hides the thin moon behind curtains of cloud
and mills its silence in rotting spruce stumps

chilled with winter rain and chided by relentless
time, never more than a moment long.

What promise did midnight ever make, but a vow to
blossom black and insist on slow passage? Dawn

never fails, but waiting starves insomniacs
lashed to their pitiful rafts and flailing at stars.

Perhaps slanted sun will reveal frost has bejeweled
the sword ferns before melting off the sparkle,

and it will be nearly enough. Maybe the owls
hunted well and are sated in their high boughs.

Maybe all that but also, maybe not. Hunger
makes us slaves, chained together on night's

desperate passage. Listen, Joe, it had to happen.
One of you would grieve heavy as the rock

rounded by water so gradually, even tomorrow
lost patience and came far too soon.

The Prayer of Joe the Ghost

1

I will lie down in the wet alder leaves
eventually, so why not now? Owls

have always been my friends and I welcome
one silently splitting the solstice dusk and

alighting, god on a branch. Six decades
and I don't have her wisdom, but time's

short so I must listen closely to currents
in her low-throated song. Here, where

a man learns animal truths, lives the only
divinity worth worship. When she hunts,

there's no mercy, nor should there be,
but her claws and beak bring quick death

without cruelty, to serve only hunger.
I'll pray to that with this airless voice

thin as the aion. The creek keeps insisting
against the rocks that won't budge,

but are nevertheless worn down. Water
from the winter sky rinses sword ferns

and skunk cabbage, flows down to the
Pacific, mixing fresh into salt.

I watch, having opened my chest
and found a garden of terrible fruits.

I have learned how fragile is breath.
Let me leave with the bird, but not now.

2

Last night the creek surged, rose up sodden
banks to harass the hanging fern. Icy rocks
are morning's warning to plant nothing yet.

I would give everything to stay, all my desires
may be stripped and I'll accept just grace, cool
rain on my burnt brain—call it the soul

if you must. Run your cosmic fingers through
my guts and tear away the bad constellations.
Bring my capsule back from the beyond

or let it gently go and then they can finally
cry. I have practiced shadowing loved ones
and am ready for eternity as invisible as

my imagination, and as light, as unreal
except at night. Meanwhile, let us agree
there is no margin in which we linger

other than memory. Give me that, then.
I have written some observations down.
Some are still singing from the shelves.

3

May the cherry tree forgive me every nail,
the saw's teeth and the spilled sap.

May crow forgive my monolingual
confession beneath the sickening elms.

May the river forgive me for the lack of rain,
borrowed to briefly wet my skin.

May the sun forgive me my shadow,
cast on the leaf I bent to trim.

May the page forgive the lesser poems,
shoes I shrugged off my stumbling feet.

May the worm forgive my endless
digging in already perfect earth.

May north wind forgive me for facing south,
broad back turned, and the curses, too.

May my children forgive my imperfect love,
into which I could not stop dipping them.

May the birds that sang up the morning
forgive me for being awake all night.

May the guitar forgive the missed chords,
the loose leads and lyricless songs.

May the pots forgive the scorched soup,
misplaced lids, the worst recipes.

May the crescent moon forgive sorrows
I hung from its exquisite tips.

May the mouse in the compost forgive me,
please, for destroying her nest of blind babes.

May my students forgive my obsession with
the music of words, the pauses between.

May each fire I lit forgive me for staring
flames down to ash in search of answers.

May my lover forgive me for any night
my hand failed to trace her sloping hip.

I forgive I forgive I forgive myself for the
song I ran out of time to sing.

Crow Grants Joe the Ghost Feathers
for Dreamtime

I don't drive and you don't fly, and though I see
better in the dark and you can talk, we witness
the same trees, the same sky, the same sea.

Let us travel there and not mind the lateness
of day, shadow you throw in moonlight,
shadow I am in the branches with this

thick beak enough to get my one word right.
In dreams, I speak all languages at once
and can teach you how to do so tonight.

I want winter rain on my feathers to rinse
sunlight from my back, make me black
again, the only color that makes sense.

In dreams, you can have what you lack.
Here are some feathers from dead brothers.
Keep them, they won't need them back.

Go solo—lovers you meet there aren't lovers.
Take offs and landings are tricky, your bed
being small, the surface rumpled covers.

Try to remember everything I've said.
I won't repeat it when you see me by day,
aloof and taunting as sunrise turns red.

Our rendezvous must always be this way,
after you surrender to sleep and accept
each darkness as a gift, yours till you die.

Joe the Ghost Plays Mandolin at New Years

Slow notes in the drizzling dawn wake one hummingbird,
then another. They hover and sip from the tuning pegs,

sustenance for the songless. Joe's fingers flare, matches on
cold frets, thick and late for the break, but fierce enough

to find the melody, pull, pull the loose thread to unravel
death. Joe makes it up as he goes, like anyone who's honest.

Mandolins make you truer if you play with the right
guitarist, one who drawls when he sings and writes songs about

omega dogs. If crow listens, may it do him some good. May he
forget what he needs to, if he hasn't already. He may envy

fretwork the way Joe envies flight, but that's conjecture.
Maybe all that cawing is a trade offer, a mystical

overture, an invitation to get on with the ordeal, a trill
as a way of waiting to run down the mandolin's neck.

All the birds in this canyon are precious to Joe. Robins
diving at the placid owl, striking over and over her

hunched back, were the boldest and angriest
creatures he's ever seen. Numb-handed and nursing

a rough gear grinding between ribs and spine,
Joe looses a tune and is grateful for music again, old

friend and refuge, given by the hands to the ears, cool
water for the last thirst, blue dawn on the first day.

Schrödinger's Ghost

Paradox, to split the shadow
into parts that separate, one

drowning in the cold surf
one stumbling over dunes

for home. One listens close
to his woman's nightmare

at dawn, aware of the vast
distance to even the closest

star throwing its newest ray
over them together in bed.

In quantum superposition
she lies there alone, grieving

into her pillow and he can't
comfort her, melting as he is

into the ocean. All possibility
must collapse into the aion

and then vanish. Isn't a ghost
just a second self-anticipating

schism? When her skin slides
over his fading form he feels

warmth, so nothing yet is lost.
Nothing is yet forbidden him.

Ghost Nocturne 6

Owl in the alder, frog in the fen,
gull over dunes, crow in the spruce,
none of them singing of ghosts.

Midwinter moon barely visits, flees
over the spiral crowns of hemlocks,
retreats beyond the bay and down.

The ocean isn't angry, no matter
what they say. Waves happen, but
don't think about what it means.

Sleep if you can until dawn.
Wake and let that light rise around
the room, bringing you with it.

Joe the Ghost Plants Garlic in the Garden, January

It's late and he knows it. Already the forest
responds to growing light, subtle slide of

dusk a little later, dawn sooner. Maybe
catch that curve and ride the back side

into July, for the bulbing. Summer is so dry
the grass looks burnt and the canyons

are tinder choked. But not tonight.
January soaks every branch, slicks

the highway, urges the creeks up. Men
die crossing the bar, one huge wave

flipping their hold full of crab, two swept
onto the beach, one trapped in the boat.

But things won't stop growing, something
Joe intimately knows in this season of

poison, time of burned tongues and
fingers on fire, of salty pain and near

prayers. He's planting cloves because love
is ending and must be offered anyway.

Ghosts taste nothing, but some flavors
still find him, all is not lost. Garlic is proof

there are gods in the soil and the sun, ones
you can eat, who will wait to eat you.

Joe the Ghost Eats Supper Alone

The barred owl refuses his
invitation and will not show her

wings' geometry in the canyon's
green dusk. Even the hummingbirds

look more desperate than in
November, when the rains linked

with rains and dimmed noon.
Psithurisms shift the Sitka round

and the creek muscles over the basalt
boulder that usually splits it.

This morning he hovered above big
surf, as if gull or kite or, finally, ghost.

Salt spray rose up into the spruce,
dissipating inland where he now

absorbs it again. The potatoes in his
soup are hot and tender in his mouth.

Peasant bread was a good choice.
He can remember what flavors

these things had, not the same as
actually tasting. Alone, he can eat

slowly, not having to speak or listen.
The owl has still not arrived and

the crows for once are silent, maybe
out of respect, but probably not.

Joe the Ghost Weakens

His ribs have begun to click when he walks, his hips
are loose and his breath, shallow. The owl
in the alder looks away, away, when he walks
out in the rain. The scent of leafmould smells
more familiar than ever and his dreams stop
at the knots. He climbs the ladder and almost
falls. It takes Joe two trips uphill with a half-full
wheelbarrow and each time he's twice as winded.
He sings while he works and, in the silence
between songs, the whispers are incessant.
The shirts that didn't fit him before now do.
Bugs fly through his face and barely notice,
though it tickles him a little. Joe is not
afraid of dying, but of the space between
living and dying. Once, as a boy, he found a
mole in the woods, late autumn as the cold
began to bite. It shivered in his dirty palm
and then, after a while, it did not.
Even a child, or especially one, knows
when he's entered the sublime. The crows
confirmed his suspicions while he dug
a shallow hole with a stick and he never forgot.

Joe the Ghost Reconsiders Rain

Rain begins beyond his reach
and falls and falls until it flows.
Nothing he's done ever increased
the chance of drought or flood,
nor blackened clouds nor piled them
high or erased them, revealing
pale blue sky. The chilled hummingbird
works harder with wet wings, incandescent
reds and greens muted by dampness.
Joe raises his face to the gray
firmament and tastes the soft salt
passing through his tongue and leaving
a trace of words: *sorrow survival*
tomorrow never forever. Inside, his woman
sits warm before the fire. His half glass of
red wine flares, a melted garnet
on the table. Slowly, so slowly, these his
comforts recede into the distance until
all that's left is scent of rain.

Ghost Nocturne 7

He hides in the forest at midnight when his
form grows most visible, feet threatening
to grow roots and capture him, wild, half-alive,

and never let him go home. There under
ancient alders, their limbs cloaked in pale
moss glowing green in the gibbous moon's

light, less strong than last night's, he will
cry for deliverance, for more chances to
get it all right. Even the finches, huddling

in their thicket of branches, will recognize
despair and listen more closely for new songs
in a minor key, a tune to tempt the sunrise

to burst sooner. One never knows
what blade will finally break through skin
and slice the soul deep enough to extinguish

that ghostly organ mistaken as magical.
He wets his throat with rain until he can taste
the sea again. He licks the grooved bark

for the flavors he forgot, having lived so long
on just the scent rising from the nape of her
neck, sustenance enough for any specter.

In the forest, lies are useless, especially those
told to the self. The owl accepts in commerce
only the coin of the realm, the honest anguish

with which we pay the biggest debts. Her eggs
are perfected from eons of effort and will hatch
even if a sad spirit makes his home beneath

her nest. Prayers mean nothing if not spoken
in the language of small gods, made of so few
words, though they're ones no human knows.

Joe the Ghost Brews a Stout

Hands will have forever
in which to lie still. Flavor

can only be tasted
with a fleshed tongue,

trembling organ that serves
both thirst and the language

of thirst, what we plunge
into our hungers and how we

tell of that immersion. A glass
of stout is a holy bath in

cocoa and burnt malt flecked
with foam. What's not to like,

even if specters can't taste
any of it, nor feel the fluid

enter their throats and chase
chill blue rain back up the sky?

Joe stirs the grain and prays
he won't fade until the beer

pours from the bourbon barrel
on a fair summer afternoon.

Scalpels Used on Ghosts

The scalpels used on ghosts are hammered
flat from the metals of meteorites,

cosmic alloys smelted in space that streaked
through the vacuum and blazed through

atmosphere, boring deep into turf to cool
in moist soil. Folded, pounded, folded,

pounded, tiny katana slowly taking shape,
always worked in moonlight by a dying

master with no apprentice to teach.
Held aloft in pure darkness, it glows blue

and whorls animate across the blade,
showing scenes from the future life of the

suffering one it will incise. These tools
are the only ones sharp enough to cleave

flesh halfway to forgetting its incarnation,
halfway to accepting it may never again

feel warmth when caressed. A scalpel
such as this weighs nothing in the surgeon's

hand. The incisions do not even bleed.
The excised tumor won't know it's been

unhoused and will carry on its hideous
divisions in the basin where it's dropped.

No ghost needs anesthesia, but some
still request it, affectless yet reassuring,

for the long surgery. Their sutures, spun
from the tails of comets, melt elegantly

away and leave a delicate trail
on skin and sky only some will witness.

Snow Falls on Joe the Ghost

Softer than rain, and quieter,
the first flake rises up the
hospital window as if escaping

Earth, refusing the inevitable
liquefaction on anonymous
streets. Once snow would melt

on his skin, but now it makes drifts
in his hair. He passes through glass
as crystals pass through him

and only those that settle
on his chest thaw. Doves swoop
in unison from eaves and flecked firs

and huddle on the other perch,
offer their soft, unceasing laments
to Joe, ghost and amanuensis.

The Future Fades from Joe the Ghost

Exotic places he would go,
the body he would hold at night
that whispers in sweet breaths
across wet cheeks, of destinations.
Sourdough's scent, cooling on a counter,
fat snowflakes landing on wet spring grass,
are worth remembering, as is the
the language of crows he almost learned.
He wants to dive from rocks into a
cold river, walking the strand at sunset,
mad gulls wheeling overhead.
He wants the snap of his dear guitarist
busting another D-string, mid song.
Also, wind in the pines, wind over dunes,
first deep swallow of cold beer for a
thirsty ghost on an endless quest.
Let the big cat purr against his chest
as he reads again the last page of his
favorite book. Let him pause at the
nape of her neck on a rainy day.
Give him the good poems he wrote,
but not the rest, the song of two owls'
soft calls in autumn dusk from the
dripping alders that are their perch.
Let him lie down once more between
cool sheets, the canyon's imperfect
silences, the memory of his first kiss
and his last, that comes too soon.

Joe the Ghost Spends a Night Alone

It rains all day, but stops at dusk so he steps outside,
stands barefoot on the wet deck and lets the chill

infuse his shins, run a shiver up his hips and spine.
A candle lit against the night brightens as darkness falls,

beckons him inside. All homes are one day abandoned,
every bed made a desert no matter how often

lovers drenched it. All bodies are given back so ghosts
learn to burn white with desire, pale hands extended

toward the beloved, asleep in a strange room, waking
and weeping, pacing the hallway, shoulders shaking.

It's better to be invisible if you're hunted or haunting,
better to be half flesh if your best dreams won't finish

or your fears reveal they're bottomless and ready.
Those who do not practice aloneness will never

survive it, will enter eternity unprepared, arms
flailing, without a voice, waiting forever for the other

to speak their name. Slowly, forgotten as is necessary,
his name replaced on her tongue, he would finally

root to one spot and lose even the solace of
wandering, forced to wait for the moon to

fill again and illuminate the glen. Joe knows this
will happen to him if he doesn't learn how to inhabit

emptiness, how to set utter silence to shimmer,
how to hear the flowing stream return as rain.

Ghost Nocturne 8

Sleep deep, let the moon paint spruces
shades of silver never meant to be seen.

The barred owl slumbers in the ancient alder
arced over the creek and will never confess

its loneliness. The ensatina salamander
clings in the cold to the slickest rock and

feels no regret nor fear of death. Wind
moans through graceful Sitka limbs, but

not because it can never leave Earth.
The ever-present rolls its lone wheel over

the sprawled bones of lovers in their beds
and circumscribes their lives so they call it time.

Come morning, they have no choice but to
see a new day, though ghosts know the truth,

that we inhabit a continuous now until
we don't. All the prayers the living utter in

despair and desire, and all the echoes they are
paid, were never going anywhere. The multiverse

is a vacuum, vast and black, where breathed
words find no air to vibrate, no deities waiting

to be named and implored. Better to give songs
to the sword ferns undulating on the slope,

to stream-water running down to the sea,
to the sea itself, making love to the shore.

Joe the Ghost in the Castle Mirror

The rain came down and the river rose
brown within its banks, and the rain

came down. Spring was the same, only swollen.
Pigeons were frantic, whether fleeing to or from

parapets, as hunting hawks flew faster.
Torn clouds hurried low over land, indifferent

to the sun they muted or released in a fractal
too huge in scale for Joe to perceive its whorls.

He accepted what light there was and the river
rose, crows in the oaks hacking en masse,

a cacophony that reached him in his tower
and became almost harmonious. He was

approaching peace by accident when he glimpsed
himself in the glass, hunched around his wound,

surprised to be incarnate still. In mirrors,
we see not the self but its inversion, hints

of the multiverse and quantum identity,
either a lie or a truth when it matters most.

Some Things Joe the Ghost Must Do

Joe must thank the owls for their welcome, screeched
before midnight, before the darkness accepted his
pale form slipping among towering spruce trunks.
He must remember to strip his now useless clothes
so he glows as he goes there, luminous, but forever
unseen. Joe must learn how to walk silently
in such a forest and leave no footprints in moss
cloaking the nurse trees, horizontal mothers
layered deeply, dissolving in measures of time the
casual hiker ignores from his poor home, ignorance.
Joe's quest is to find the moonlight's
vertical, marginless shaft in a clearing and
bathe in phosphor to be clean for the journey.
Joe must sing a death song in tones not known
by the living so they will actually listen for once
with their inner ear, the one they tune to their gods
of broken promises who offer false fantastic things
without end, drowning out the sonorous, subtle real.
Joe must praise the worm and the beetle who will
finally flense the vestiges of his weighted body,
thus releasing him. He must master then the language
given only to the truly gone, who speak to no one
the necessary wisdom that always goes unheard.

Dreams of Joe the Ghost

1

Hairless flesh stretched over bulging
muscles, it strains against its chain, taut
and quivering. Its one fang gleams or

does it glow, since there's no light
and never has been in this wood. Clearly,
it's hungry, but can it ever be sated?

What god, imagined by men, invented
a beast like this? It sets to gnashing
in the softest, warmest glen and soon

its face will be bathed in blood, the sound
of its working jaws bearable only to
a deaf ghost, which he is not.

2

Skating glossy ice he glimpses a crater's
jagged edge drifted with moondust. Crows

crossing sky appear on the surface with
white outlines and caws reversed, an

awkward intake on the closing consonant.
Spruce line the pond, point second selves

into its depths, their crowns diving, but
frozen midway. His skates cut their

first lines and he remembers to listen to
ice sing at the touch, hear his strides' tight

bowstrokes, the hard stop's rough gouge,
the slow glide's fading low note.

His breath in frigid air no longer billows
in clouds. The wind does not toss his

hair round his face, though neither does it
chill his ears. In the morning, his thighs

will not burn, not even softly in that
pleasant way, when he descends stairs.

The last light in a lakeshore house goes dark.
He'll skate alone all night again, no need to

visit the dark, shuttered warming hut
to drink a cold cup of hot chocolate.

Near dawn he'll sit and unlace his skates,
but he won't lean across the car seat to

kiss his mother when she picks him up,
since she won't, not even in a ghost's dream.

3

The rowboat tethered at the dock rests
not in the water but above it, still
as no boat ever. With a toe he tests

the lake and loses balance, his fall
ungraceful and immersion a shock.
In their dreams, ghosts can feel

again, which some consider luck
and others a curse. He sinks lower
and comes to rest, head on a rock.

Overhead, sun makes a shadow bower
of the boat, beckoning him to rise,
floating the last of life as a lure.

He swims up toward the jewels in the skies
from that place ancient as poems,
soon to return, those jewels in his eyes.

Crows Comfort Joe the Ghost

The surgeons unsealed him where there was
no seam, took a long look and turned from the task,

sure there was no cure, and they stapled him up.
Photos showed his guts were fading, some organs'

outlines diffuse even under the operating room's
intense white lights. Did they recite a surgeon's prayer

in their retreat? Did they recognize he'd turned
more ghost than man and was now beyond anything

they could do with fine steel tools and human hands?
He was delivered back to the animals who know

how to die. In their realm, one falls to earth and begins
again to become it, the body which has lost rendering

itself to soil and wind, aided by rain, made whole again
with its birth. Joe lay days in white sheets under a flock of

kind nurses who nevertheless brought endless needles
and searched and searched for his disappearing veins,

asked repeatedly of his pain, which they smothered,
and he was grateful. Then came the black birds,

circling the parapet, cawing his new name, furious
in their remonstrations of death. It was this that

freed him, not from grief, but from its un-nameable
sheath, the negating one that would enclose him, make

a prisoner of the man. Joe remembered how the crows
followed him home as a boy, alighting on each elm

just ahead and calling, as if he'd forgotten the way,
as if he needed their voices to coax and guide him.

Ghost Bear

His impulse is to run. The worst thing
you can do, even if your spectral self is fast
as wind, is flee. Joe the Ghost sees her
bulk atop the boulder, silver sheen round the
dish-shaped face a halo or a portal
through which he'll pass. He knows the bear
knows him and has been waiting just here,
beside the lone trail up the mountain.
Perspiration leaves his silhouette like mist
from a cascade, upward in canyon shadows,
dissipating in shafts of sun. Joe watches her
nose twitch, sees her bounce several times
on her front legs, huge shoulders hunching
in preparation for use. His impulse again
is to run, cartwheel down the steepest
slope, snagging on saplings and rocks,
shedding the last of his flesh, the part
no ghost bear will ever consume.
Hibernating all his life, she now has
come forth, hungry in a spiritual way.
He was warned at the trailhead and
chose to laugh, and he laughs now
differently, having finally understood
as she moves toward him, shivering among
splashed wildflowers. She does not hurry.
Crow caws in the tree behind him,
a ragged taunt softened at the end with
sympathy, which is new. Somewhere
behind the drape of pines, water
insists on falling to a pool that cannot
stop brimming. Joe realizes it's spring,
significant to everything but him.
He hopes only for the scent of sage
underfoot to calm him, bring him
ready into her arms for the rending.

Ghost Nocturne 9

Dawn infuses pale blue behind the canyon rim, spruce
outlined as if hoarding darkness. Whatever is lost

in daylight will return with dusk. Even haunting has
limits, though no ghost knows this. If stars fade

as sky slowly brightens, it's our eyes that fail, not
their fires. The owls are done hunting and perch

on alder branches to rest and watch sunrise. Raider
Jays are content to wait, knowing just where the

robins' eggs are. The creek keeps insisting on
gravity and singing of the sea it seeks and the rocks

it smoothes, recalibrating time as it flows. Any man
who steps out of time, by choice or force, learns

to measure it differently, as a circle. The worst
ghost is more permanent than the best man,

more at peace with the gouge tip of loss working
at his wood. The sun has not burned through its

fuel, the rising light proves, and for this the birds
are ecstatic, and they go mad with melodies

in the patch of red elderberries. A ghost chorus
intones, muffled by its rising up from forest duff.

Whatever night had to say, it must wait to finish.
For a while, blue deepens and the ghosts can rest.

Joe the Ghost at Dawn Again

And how the birds sing, so sure of spring,
convinced dawn is coming, and it must.
Mostly finches and robins, but here's the thing—

if the crows had a song they would confuse
even themselves by singing about the palest
blue behind the spruce, how it can infuse

black sky, obscuring stars, revealing the forest
as anything but impenetrable. But they wait
in silence, warming black fledglings in the nest,

content to let songbirds take up the debate
over darkness and light. Still corporeal,
Joe just wants to set the record straight.

His dreams, neither celestial nor arboreal,
tend to cease at the crisis and he always wakes
on Earth, subject to gravity, un-sartorial.

All ghosts go forth nude, but no one speaks
of this. He clings to his body this morning,
fading feet and hands dancing with dull sparks.

Being born should come with a warning
that regardless of your gods, it comes to this—
the desire to live on that just keeps burning.

Ghost Tattoo

When morning black broke it leaked
pale blue and pink, refused an ending

to night's last dream. His ghost tattoo
grew invisible in the light.

The cafe in town was closed. He ate breakfast
from his palm with pigeons under a bridge.

You may ask, what was it he hoped
to accomplish with his dagger and list

of grievances, what ink could ever
render anger indelible.

Haunted absent image, he learned
how pierced flesh felt, the raw red

welt for in which a secret could dwell,
anchorite in her dark cell, an ideal

that won't age though the skin will.
Never underestimate regret nor

how some wounds almost heal.
The only holy moment is always

happening, as wind flees up a
steep slope of dawn-lit spruce.

Joe the Ghost and the Beach Picnic

Mermen wrestle in the aqua curve of
breakers muscling over against rock,
exploding in spray. Their immortality

is mythic, suspect, but they swim
so powerfully he can't doubt some
magic at work. If they die, their bones

are reinhabited among bright coral.
The ocean permits no haunting
and the beaches are already full.

On a May afternoon, south wind
strong but warm, and sun abundant,
he doesn't believe in ghosts. One cold

beer later he still believes only in
the salt air engulfing him, sand hot
between his fingers, her laughter.

His sandwich is the best sandwich ever.
Heavy waves thud, chthonic
commentary that takes years

he doesn't have. But these cherries,
will you just try them, they are
so sweet, so good, right now.

Joe The Ghost Shares His Bread with Crow

Once Joe grows still, quiets first
his hands then his mind, Crow
comes down from the shore pine,
takes his place on a fence rail,
black as ever, nonchalant about
proximity, pretending Joe is
fully ghosted, harmless.
It's not true and both know, but
friendship between winged and
wingless requires shadow trust,
an unspoken promise to keep
a respectful distance. Crow's hunger
is not like Joe's, which only grows
for immaterial fruits, time
measured in years, touch of the
beloved in dreams, a bag
big enough to hold all the loss.
The sandwich in his lap is
pointless, bread stale as regret,
imagined flavor imaginary.
Crow waits, pacing the rail
toward the breaking waves
and back, reciting his reductive
philosophy which comes down
to this—bread belongs to the
hungriest one, the survivor.

The Library of Joe the Ghost

Some libraries, awash in sun or under
glass domes, hold secrets even ghosts
don't know. Some the ivy climbs,

cheating through windows at night
just to read the spines. Some libraries
are memories, their contents lost,

scattered dust, books that deserved it
and books that didn't. Joe's is not
Alexandria's. The ghost of Herodotus

has not thumbed Stan's *False Prophet*
nor has Plato borrowed Blake's
Songs of Innocence and Experience,

not that he would. Joe's library
represents what his brain grew
fat on, what built the boy into a

madman wrestling words to a draw.
Bishop is content to lean against Burns,
Plath against Pessoa, and Welsh not-twins

RS and Dylan Thomas sit unwilling
to touch but in awe of each other
on the shelf forever. Who knew

Rimbaud and Roethke would find
common ground but stranger still
are Merwin, Milosz, and Montale

slinging their several languages
in animated exchange. At night,
the bookcase glows subtly blue

from the energy of implied
metaphors bound and unable to
test the edges of vagueness.

Joe puts them in boxes, horizontal
after years of verticality and words
cling to their pages against gravity

and time, as if the order matters
and the poets were finally right. Each
lies still, as usual.

Somewhere, an eye and an ear,
a keen mind and a soft
imagination, await the gifts.

Somewhere, the poets will sing
again, sing like they dld for Joe,
sing like they might die tomorrow.

Ghost Finch

All along, it was the yellow finch
that sharp retort a counterpoint to
mellifluous songs of robins, doves.

High summer, top heavy, leans
into August, the saddest sunsets
and the sweetest blackberries

high up the thorny slope. Wind's
work will never end, nor the rain's.
Two creeks will merge and flow

for the ocean. The sick finch will
drop from the branch and the other
birds will all sing to its ghost.

The Burning House of Joe the Ghost

1

We are made to burn, as are our homes. Crow
builds a nest and her nest burns. The planet

burns while we pretend it's a lie. Joe's house
is made of wood from the forest, fine grained

and richly stained. In fact, a spark lit the blanket
years ago so this is slow, or was, until now.

His first bucket of water is blown back at him
by the flames. His next fills slower while heat

climbs the walls. The broadsides and paintings
burn musically, and in colors. Rooms

surrender, one after another. What happened
in each is now mute. It's almost beautiful

how the white flames burst the bed
and all the perfumes their bodies abandoned

make sweet smoke. Joe's got so little flesh
he can walk through the fire and it only

hurts a little. The rare wood of the hutch
is consumed by the blue blaze-dancers. Down

come the curling family photos, down
come the walls themselves.

2

Maybe it started in the kitchen, the aptly named
Ghost peppers pyromaniacal in the gut.

Once a flame ignited, there was plenty of fuel.
Sleepers on the upper floors felt their dreams

become brighter and warmer. Joe dreamt of a
beach where the chill blue ocean turned

slowly aqua and he was buoyant.
Smoke gathered under the stairs and then

disgorged itself, spilling across the ceiling
and from every seam. He awoke when flames

came from his hands, where the last nerves
gave their lives. How the drapes burned. How

the books burned, the best ones first,
curling back and blackening, page by page.

When he doused the carpet by the bed,
it steamed. He wet down their bed—

how could she still be asleep!—and next
the cat, unsuccessfully. His shelf of

manuscripts sagged and smoked. He tried
to save the slimmest but overnight it had

grown too heavy to lift. Crows screaming
from the pines could be taken a couple of ways.

Fire's beauty manifests as it burns the ineffable.
Joe's house was always a metaphor, as was Joe.

The Herbalist Treats Joe the Ghost

The first thing she says is, "I cannot
un-ghost you so don't ask." This covers

a lot of ground, answers the main
question he has: "Must it be now?"

Her green hands have missing fingers
so she has her own ghosts. Waxy bottles

tilt on her shelf, opaque liquids angled,
pseudolatinate names on labels.

Her dusty old books have pages
of recipes that include nonexistent

substances. Her hands tremble when she
stirs them into a vial of orange oil. Joe

retrieves his wallet and chooses bills
he can see through. If magic blooms

in his cells, if he stops fading and feels
re-fleshed, he'll return with the other kind.

Joe the Ghost's Enormous Coat

It used to fit. The zipper opened easily
to the universe and the collar was warm
on his neck. Now wind finds its way

up the sleeves and rain paints epaulets
on the shoulders. Joe's once broad back
went bony and the coat hangs loose. He has

no use for a coat, but on a drizzling day
people will wonder why he goes out
in just a shirt. What nerves he had are numb.

Sunburn is less of a problem, as are
mosquitos. This was Joe's favorite coat,
light enough for an autumn walk.

He puts it on, feels like a kid wearing
his father's jacket, leather soft and
aromatic. Joe rolls up the cuffs and

tightens his belt so his pants won't slip
off his hips. It's getting ridiculous.
As he grows weightless, will he finally

learn to fly? He wants to be a platinum
shadow on a full moon night,
neither coat against cold nor feathers.

Joe the Ghost at Summer's End

Wind blows differently all of a sudden, lifts
shore-pines' limbs and lets them fall as it

whips around the dunes. If summer were
endless, he'd hate that worse than the yellow

tone infusing the alders along the river.
The hillsides are spread with grass so dry

it shatters under his weightless footfall.
If one has to come to an agreement with

death, shouldn't it be signed as light fails
early, as Fall seduces him to love the

low-angle sun. Joe notes the grasshoppers
no longer notice him and the swallows

keep darting through his ribs like the
whole thing is a joke. It's not, but he still

laughs when the moon pulls his hair
or he hears Crow first, at dawn, ranting

about a new problem with the same old
caw he always uses. Joe isn't fooled.

His limitless visiting rights will allow him
to haunt autumn until he's had his fill.

He'll disappear, but won't lose his own
vision. Summer may be over, but the Sun

has work left and promised to return. Joe
will be back, a trick of light, a lantern.

Joe the Ghost Argues All Night

Mainly, it's a quarrel with himself, one that hinges
in the middle and is never a fair fight. Someone
has to lose more than half the time. He advocates

for one view or the other, keeps noticing the
family resemblance. Eventually, all ghosts come
to the same conclusion—only the empty are

invisible and the rest carry what they can't let go,
leaving traces wherever they haunt. The worst,
the obsessed, can't help but materialize and escape

through narrow portals. Joe will learn to live
with that. He'll write precisely no more poems
about it. Willed silence is not the same as silence,

though identical and similarly broken
with a word or a sound allowed only the living.
His friends will have to write the poems then.

Joe the Ghost Bids His Friends Farewell

There is a moment when the red-tailed hawk
leans forward from the fencepost, tense wings furled.

The flight will be brief, over the meadow first,
over the hemlocks twisting tips, over mossy

Sitka spruce whose muscled roots burrow
into the ravine to hold the creek's banks

in place. Finally, at the high ridge he'll catch
a thermal, wide turning on the wind until he

tops the firs and sees the ocean curving
perfectly away, blue-green under gold sun.

Acknowledgments

MCP and the Executors of Chris Ransick estate humbly recognize that some poems from this collection, in present or previous versions, may have formerly appeared in other publications individually, but have no present knowledge of such. We ask that if there are any publication acknowledgments for any of these poems known by readers, that they please contact Middle Creek Publishing so that such acknowledgment may be present in future printings of this title. Thank you.

Special gratitude to both Michael Henry and Lighthouse Writers Workshop for the impetus and generosity in the acquiring and release of this book.

Gratitude to the Denver literary community, Chris Ransick's family, fans and readers from the region and beyond.

About the Author

Chris Ransick, Denver Poet Laureate from 2006-2010, was an award winning author of six books of poetry and fiction. He was born and raised in upstate New York and lived in Colorado, Montana, Wyoming, California, and Oregon. He worked as a journalist, editor, professor, and speaker and served on his city's public library board, his state's humanities board of directors, and on the PEN Freedom to Write Committee. His first book, *Never Summer*, won a 2003 Colorado Book Award for Poetry. His book of short stories, *A Return to Emptiness*, was a 2005 Colorado Book Award for fiction finalist. His stories and poems have been presented on television, radio, and stage, including collaborations with Ballet Nouveau Colorado. He was a faculty member from 2005-2019 at Lighthouse Writers Workshop, Denver's independent creative writing school. Lighthouse awarded him the 2013 Beacon Award for Teaching Excellence. Chris held his final reading at Lighthouse Writers Workshop on September 25, 2019.

ABOUT MIDDLE CREEK PUBLISHING

MIDDLE CREEK PUBLISHING believes that responding to the world through art & literature — and sharing that response — is a vital part of being an artist.

MIDDLE CREEK PUBLISHING is a company seeking to make the world a better place through both the means and ends of publishing. We are publishers of quality literature in any genre from authors and artists, both seasoned and as-yet undervalued, with a great interest in works which may be considered to be, illuminate or embody any aspect of contemplative Human Ecology, defined as the relationship between humans and their natural, social, and built environments.

MIDDLE CREEK's particular interest in Human Ecology, is meant to clarify an aspect of the quality in the works we will consider for publication and is meant as a guide to those considering submitting work to us. Our interest is in publishing works illuminating the Human experience through words, story or other content that connects us to each other, our environment, our history, and our potential deeply and more consciously.

www.ingramcontent.com/pod-product-compliance
Lightning Source LLC
Chambersburg PA
CBHW062119080426
42734CB00012B/2921